WILDFLOWERS
OF SEQUOIA & KINGS CANYON
NATIONAL PARKS

BY
STEPHEN K. STOCKING & JACK A. ROCKWELL

**Sequoia
Natural History
Association**

**HCR 89 Box 10
Three Rivers
California, 93271
USA**

FIRST EDITION 1969
SECOND EDITION 1989
THIRD EDITION 1999

ISBN 1-878441-08-6
Printed in the United States

*   *   *   *   *   *   *   *   *   *   *   *

PUBLISHED BY
THE SEQUOIA NATURAL HISTORY ASSOCIATION

The non-profit Sequoia Natural History Association works in partnership with the National Park Service to provide educational publications and programs for Sequoia and Kings Canyon National Parks and Devils Postpile National Monument. For a publications catalog or information on membership, field seminars and other educational programs, call (559) 565-3759 or e-mail: a-seqnha@inreach.com

Internet web page http://www.sequoiahistory.org

Table of Contents

Introduction

A deeper understanding of the environment can heighten your enjoyment and make more meaningful your travels. This philosophy, not a need to classify or accumulate, is the reason for this publication of the wildflowers of Sequoia and Kings Canyon National Parks.

Here the visitor may travel from an elevation of 2,000 feet to 7,600 feet without leaving park highways. Taking to the trails, you may climb as high as the summit of Mount Whitney, 14,495 feet, and still encounter wildflowers. Within the more than 1,300 square miles of Sequoia and Kings Canyon National Parks, there are many ecological areas from grassland and chaparral to alpine areas above timberline. Each area has different conditions which make it suitable for the growth of different varieties of flowering plants. There are more than 1500 species of flowering trees, shrubs and wildflowers within this diverse area.

The flora of the Sierra Nevada has had a long time to develop. Plants from many areas immigrated to the Sierra Nevada during different periods of geologic time when conditions were ideal. As conditions changed with the passage of time, plants either adapted to the new conditions or died out. This is another reason for the great diversity of the flora. Some of the plants of the east side of the Sierra Nevada are adapted to very dry conditions. As the Sierra Nevada rose through time, a dry area developed on the east side. As the climate of this part of California changed to one of wet winters and dry summers the plants had to

adapt to these conditions or they could not survive. Within this general area there are also other environmental conditions to which plants must be adapted. The most important of these is the difference in length of growing season from the foothills to the Sierra crest. This varies from 6 to 10 months in the low chaparral country to a few weeks in the alpine areas. Because of these varying conditions, some plants reach their northern-most distribution in Kings Canyon National Park and others reach their southern limit in the high mountains of Sequoia National Park. Many foothill species are widespread in similar areas of northern and southern California. A few plants are found only within the limits of the two parks, but these are few as the habitats here are duplicated in other areas of California. An increasing number of weedy species compose the most recent group of plants to arrive within the parks.

For convenience, we will divide the plants of the parks into three groups, those of low, middle and high elevations. Many of the plants of low elevation will be seen only by those who visit the foothills in the parks in the spring. Most summer visitors will see the plants of the middle elevations, as it is here that roads and campgrounds are located.

To see the flowers of the high elevations, it will be necessary to take to the trails for a hike of a day or longer. For your convenience a description of these three areas follows. The place names used here are marked on road signs and on local maps.

LOW ELEVATIONS:

Below approximately 4,000 feet.

The majority of the plants of this area bloom from March to early June. Some parts of this area are cloaked by chaparral while others are covered by foothill woodland. Chaparral, or brush, is found below 4,000 feet on highway 180 between General Grant Grove and Fresno. On highway 198 between Grant Forest and Three Rivers, it occurs downward from Deer Ridge and Amphitheater Point. The road to Mineral King passes through miles of chaparral. The other area in which many of these low elevation flowers are found is on highway 180 between General Grant Grove and Cedar Grove. On this road, extensive chaparral vegetation occurs between the area just below the turnoff to Hume Lake and the vicinity of Grizzley Creek Falls in the Kings Canyon.

MIDDLE ELEVATIONS:

Between approximately 4,000 and 7,000 feet.

Most of the plants of this area bloom from June to August. This is the area of Sequoia-Kings Canyon National Parks most seen by summer visitors because here are located the giant sequoia groves and the campgrounds of Lodge-pole, Grant Grove and Cedar Grove. This area is called the yellow pine forest but often the most common tree is the white fir. Most of the Generals Highway is in this middle elevation forest as are the areas above Snowline Lodge on highway 180 and above Deer Ridge on highway 198. Occasionally the Generals Highway gets up into the red fir forest which is considered to be the beginning of the high elevations. Yellow pine forest is also found at Atwell Mill in the south part of Sequoia National Park and at Cedar Grove in the Kings Canyon.

HIGH ELEVATIONS:

Above 7,000 feet.

The majority of the plants of this area bloom from July to September. Only the lowest parts of this area can be seen from the road, but most of the extensive backcountry of the two parks is made up of red fir forest, lodgepole forest, subalpine forest and alpine fell-fields, or areas above timberline. These areas are quite different, but will be considered together for the purposes of this book.

The lower parts of this area can be seen on the Generals Highway at Big Baldy Saddle and Little Baldy Saddle as well as in Tokopah Valley and at Wolverton Meadow. It can also be reached by the trails to Alta Peak, Heather Lake and Twin Lakes which start in the Giant Forest area. Mineral King gives superb examples of high elevation areas. Between the parks in Sequoia National Forest, the Big Meadows area affords entrance to high elevation. In General Grant Grove some plants of this area are seen on Park Ridge. Soon after leaving the trailheads on the east side of the parks the high elevations are reached.

It should be remembered that the range of plants characteristic of lower elevations extends upward on the warmer, drier, south facing slopes and that high elevation plants are often found at low elevations on the cool, damp north facing slopes.

The plants included in this book are among the most common in these parks and have been grouped according to color to help you in their identification. For those who are interested in a more complete listing of the plants, we have compiled a checklist of park plants which can be seen at park interpretive offices. When a flower is found that is not included here you can refer to the other books mentioned in the references or consult with a naturalist at any of the visitor centers. To describe a plant it is helpful to remember the type of location in which the flower was seen, meadow or forest, etc., as well as the flower color and other characteristics of the plant.

The common names used here are those which are generally accepted. It should be remembered that common names vary from area to area and are not standardized in usage. For this reason other common names are often included in the descriptions. For the scientific name the standard reference work on California plants has been used: *The Jepson Manual Higher Plants of California*. Edited by James C. Hickman. Quite often more than one species of a genus occurs within the parks, in these cases one of the most common types is pictured and described and others may be mentioned. The partial descriptions attempt to describe the plants through distinguishing characteristics. We have also mentioned the habitat, meadow . . . forest . . . etc., and the elevations at which the plants are found. In addition, other interesting notes about early and present day uses of the plants are often included.

Appreciation for comments and suggestions on improving the original text go to former Chief Park Naturalist R. K. Grater,, former Ass't Chief Park Naturalist R. C. Burns and Dr. J. Arnold of Sonoma State College. Contributions of photographs other than those made by the authors and from park files were made by R. K. Grater, R. C. Burns, Robert Zink, Maurice Zardus and C. Mack Shaver. Title page and back page artwork by Janene Richert.

Please remember that this is a national park, a natural preserve for all those who will visit here. Take only pictures, and we hope a store of wonderful memories goes home with you; but leave all else for the enjoyment of others.

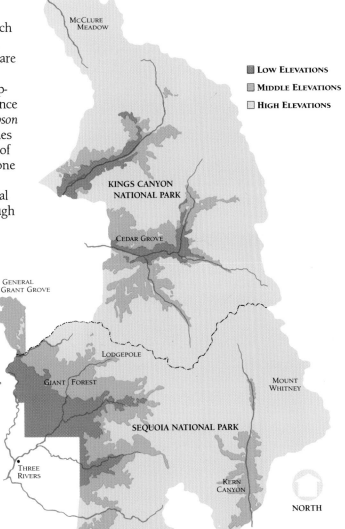

Live Forever   April–June

Golden Ear-Drops   April–September

Rabbitbrush   August–October

Common Madia   March–June

Common Monkeyflower   March–August

Dudleya cymosa
STONECROP FAMILY

LIVE FOREVER

These plants are familiar to most of us as some of the species are extensively cultivated in our gardens as border plants. Because of their habit of producing a circle of young plants around the parent, they are commonly called hen and chickens. With numerous fleshy basal leaves, rock lettuce, as it sometimes called, blooms on warm, rocky outcroppings from April through June.

Dicentra chrysantha
POPPY FAMILY

GOLDEN EAR-DROPS

During the summer months the tall stems of this yellow *Dicentra* can be found on dry slopes, disturbed places and on burns below 5,000 feet. The stems bear loose clusters of golden blossoms, perched erect instead of drooping like the closely related bleeding hearts. The finely dissected pale and shiny green leaves, often a foot or more long, seem unusually graceful in contrast to the stiff stems.

Bleeding heart, *D. formosa* with deep-purple flowers, can be found in damp and shaded places as at Crystal Cave. Steers head, *D. uniflora* with small, white or pink flowers, is found in gravelly and rocky places from red fir forests up to an elevation of 12,000 feet.

Chrysothamnus nauseosus ssp. *albicaulis*
SUNFLOWER FAMILY

RABBITBRUSH

Rabbitbrush is a small evergreen shrub found in dry flats and open areas. It is common on the east slope of the Sierra and in similar areas on the western slope, often growing to elevations of 9,000 feet. The small flowers are clustered at the top of this brittle shrub. The word *Chrysothamnus* is Greek for "gold shrub." Some species of *Chrysothamnus* contain a milky latex and have been considered as rubber substitutes in the past.

Closely related to this group is *Ericameria*, goldenbush, which also blooms in late summer. Both *Chrysothamnus* and *Ericameria* have many bushy species that reside in dry habitats. Both are members of the aster tribe of the sunflower family.

Madia elegans
SUNFLOWER FAMILY

COMMON MADIA

Of the 7 known species of *Madia* found within the parks, the common madia is the one most often seen along roadsides on rather dry slopes. On close observation this plant, with its sticky leaves and stems, has an odor disagreeably suggestive of turpentine. A closely related species furnishes an oil used abroad in cooking that many believe to be superior in taste to olive oil.

Mimulus guttatus
FIGWORT FAMILY

COMMON MONKEYFLOWER

Perhaps there is no more common sierran wildflower and certainly none is more widespread than this monkeyflower. It is found in seepages, meadows, and on stream banks from the lowest to the highest elevations in the parks and it takes many different sizes and leaf forms. At times the succulent leaves have been used as salad greens. The name *Mimulus* refers to the two lipped flowers with the monkey face of a comic actor.

There are many other species of this genus with flowers of various colors and combinations of colors. One of these species, *M. moschatus*, grows close to the ground in wet areas and can be recognized by its cool, clammy basal leaves and yellow flowers.

Blazing Star   *June–October*

St. John's Wort   *June–August*

Bush Senecio   *May–October*

Leopard Lily   *July–August*

California Bay   *December–May*

Hypericum formosum var. *scouleri*
ST. JOHN'S WORT FAMILY

ST. JOHN'S WORT

The name St. John's wort was given to these plants because some species were supposed to have flowered on St. John's birthday. At one time it was thought that these plants gave protection against lightning and had the property of revealing the presence of witches. The yellow flowers and translucent dotted leaves characterize this plant which is found along stream banks and in other wet places.

A low growing relative of similar situations is called tinker's penny, *H. anagalloides*. An introduced relative, klamathweed, *H. perforatum*, is poisonous to livestock but has been eliminated from most of California through the introduction of leaf eating beetles.

Lilium kelleyanum
LILY FAMILY

LEOPARD LILY

Our most common species of tiger or leopard lily grows in wet meadows and along streams at middle and high elevations. The stems stand from 1 to 6 feet in height with the color of the flowers varying from orange-yellow to almost red. Both the nodding flowers and the long leaves are arranged in whorls.

The similar *L. pardalinum* forms colonies on stream banks but is found at lower elevations while other, less common, species are found in dry areas.

Mentzelia laevicaulis
LOASA FAMILY

BLAZING STAR

Look for the cactus-like flowers of the blazing star along roadsides in places that are disturbed, dry and gravelly in the chaparral areas of both parks. Another, perhaps more appropriate name for the blazing stars as a group is stickleaf, as the plants are furnished with barbed hairs which cause them to cling to whatever they come in contact with.

Mentzelia crocea, another species with large yellow showy flowers can be found blooming earlier in similar places.

Senecio flaccidus var. *douglasii*
SUNFLOWER FAMILY

BUSH SENECIO

The bush senecio begin flowering in the late spring but may go unnoticed among the profusion of other yellow flowers blooming at the same time. However, in late summer and fall, when most other foothill flowers have finished blooming, we still find the bush senecio flowering. Finely dissected leaves covered with white hairs distinguish this species.

This plant will be encountered throughout the chaparral areas, primarily along park roadsides, up to elevations of 5,000 feet.

Umbellularia californica
LAUREL FAMILY

CALIFORNIA BAY

One will surely never forget the strong pungent odor given off by the leathery, shiny leaves of this evergreen tree. The small greenish-yellow flowers, which bloom during late winter and spring, mature into solitary fruits which turn dark purple in late summer. Usually found in canyons and valleys below 5,000 feet throughout the parks, this tree has had many uses through the years. The fruits have been roasted and eaten; the oil from seeds and leaves used for toothache, earache and patent medicines; the leaves used to cure headaches and rheumatism, and for seasoning of stews, roasts, etc.

In the same family as sassafras, cinnamon and avocado, the tree is also called pepperwood, Oregon myrtle, balm of heaven, sassafras laurel, California olive and California laurel.

Western Wall Flower   March–July

Golden Brodiaea   March–May

California Poppy   February–September

Bush Poppy   April–August

Bush Monkeyflower   April–July

Erysimum capitatum
MUSTARD FAMILY

WESTERN WALL FLOWER

In late spring and early summer we find the coarse-stemmed wall flower along park roadsides in the yellow pine forest. It is sometimes called blister cress due to the ability of the plant's juice to draw blisters. Its globe-like clusters of flowers exhibit a wide range of color from plant to plant, varying from light lemon yellow to a dark orange brown.

A subspecies, *E. capitatum* ssp. *perenne* is found at higher elevations.

Dendromecon rigida
POPPY FAMILY

BUSH POPPY

The bush poppy can be seen on the Generals Highway above park headquarters and along highway 180 between Grant Grove and Squaw Valley. It is the only true shrubby plant in the poppy family which includes some 200 species. Look for this evergreen shrub, with flowers 1 to 3 inches across, on dry slopes, stony washes, on burns and disturbed areas in the foothills in late spring and midsummer.

Triteleia ixioides ssp. *scabra*
LILY FAMILY

GOLDEN BRODIAEA

Like other brodiaeas the golden brodiaea has basal, grass-like, leaves. The flowers are on a long stalk and are shaped like small six-rayed stars. This variety is found in open sandy areas at low and middle elevations while another variety ssp. *analina*, much the same in appearance, is found in the higher mountain areas.

Along with other brodiaeas, the corms of this plant were eaten by local Indians. Seeing the Indian women digging corms, the miners misnamed the California Indians "Diggers."

Eschscholzia californica
POPPY FAMILY

CALIFORNIA POPPY

First collected by the Russian botanist Echscholtz in 1824, our state flower has been widely cultivated for its beauty. Four petals form deep orange to yellow cups which grace the sunny foothills of the "Golden State" often covering entire fields.

All members of the group *Eschscholzia* have a watery juice which possesses something of the narcotic property that distinguishes its famous oriental cousin the opium poppy. The California Indians knew of its pain killing properties and made use of the fresh root to stop the ache of a hollow tooth, while an extract from it had some vogue as a liniment to relieve headache. The foliage was sometimes cooked as a vegetable. Among Spanish Californians, the California poppy had a reputation for making the hair grow. The petals were mixed with olive oil or suet, cooked over a slow fire, strained and rubbed, in fullness of faith, on thinning hair.

At low elevations the unusual wind poppy, *Stylomecon heterophylla*, with dark red-orange flowers and the more common small frying pans, *E. lobbii*, are occasionally seen.

Mimulus aurantiacus
FIGWORT FAMILY

BUSH MONKEYFLOWER

This monkeyflower takes the form of a small evergreen shrub and has light green leaves which are sticky above and fuzzy beneath. The colors of the monkey-faced flowers vary but are often light orange-yellow. These large flowers are arranged singly in the leaf axils. Because of these characteristics this shrub is called either the sticky, or bush monkeyflower. It can be seen on rocky areas and road banks of the chaparral country.

Tarweed   *July–November*

California Goldenrod   *July–October*

Flannel Bush   *May–June*

Mountain Violet   *April–June*

Fiddleneck   *March–June*

Holocarpha heermannii
SUNFLOWER FAMILY

TARWEED

In late July and August the tarweed starts blooming along park roadsides. The leaves and stems are sticky with glandular hairs which makes the plant unpleasant to handle and forms the basis for the common name tarweed. When the herbage is crushed a distinctive spicy odor is evident.

Two other species, *H. virgata* and *H. obconica* can be found in similar habitats blooming about the same time.

Solidago californica
SUNFLOWER FAMILY

CALIFORNIA GOLDENROD

California goldenrod and other species of *Solidago* are often the last flowers to bloom in drying meadow margins and along roadsides in late summer. In the parks we have different species at low and high elevations, but all have small flowers in bright yellow heads. Like many other yellow flowers, the goldenrods have been wrongly accused of causing hayfever. Many species of goldenrod are found throughout the United States.

Fremontodendron californicum
CACAO FAMILY

FLANNEL BUSH

A striking profusion of large flowers decorate this bush through spring and into early summer. Found in disturbed and rocky areas, the shrub is often seen growing from roadside rock clefts. The surface of the plant is covered by an irritating fuzz of hairs. In the past the slippery, sticky inner bark was brewed to relieve irritations of the throat. Because of its beauty it has been widely cultivated.

Other names include fremontia and slippery elm. It is named for the explorer, General Fremont, whose party discovered it while crossing the Sierra.

Viola purpurea
VIOLET FAMILY

MOUNTAIN VIOLET

Of the 23 species of violets occurring in California about 12 are represented in these parks and of this number 9, have yellow flowers.

The mountain or pine violet is found in dryish places in the middle and high elevation forest. The petals are a deep lemon yellow with the upper two petals purplish on the back. There are several other species with this characteristic but they differ in leaf shape, altitudinal range or habitat.

In the mountain meadows and wet areas of the middle and high elevation areas one finds the stream violet, *V. glabella*, the western dog violet, *V. aduca* and the white Macloskey's violet, *V. macloskeyi*.

Amsinckia menziesii var. *intermedia*
BORAGE FAMILY

FIDDLENECK

An extremely variable species, the fiddleneck is one of the most common weedy plants of fields and open slopes of the Pacific states during early spring. The individual blossoms, attractive in color and shape, are interestingly arranged in a closely coiled inflorescence, which unwinds as the flowers open in succession along the flowering stem. The curling habit of the opening flower head somewhat resembles the neck of a violin.

Along with the popcorn flower, fiddleneck often gives a spectacular mass effect to foothill fields.

Single Stemmed Butterweed   May–August

Balsamroot   *April–June*

Meadow Lotus   *May–September*

Bigelow's Sneezeweed   June–August

Sierra Columbine   *June–August*

Senecio integerrimus var. *major*
SUNFLOWER FAMILY

SINGLE STEMMED BUTTERWEED

Groundsel, or butterweed, so called because of the yellow flowers, is a common summer flower of the open forest at middle elevations. The scientific name *Senecio* means old man and refers to the crown of soft white hairs on the wind borne fruit. There are many common species of Senecio, some of which contain alkaloids which may cause liver damage to livestock and wildlife.

Another common species is *S. triangularis*, a large plant of wet meadows and stream banks. This brilliant plant has long triangular leaves and a flat-topped head of flowers.

Helenium bigelovii
SUNFLOWER FAMILY

BIGELOW'S SNEEZEWEED

No other flower adds so much to the color of our meadows as the Bigelow's sneezeweed. A more pleasing name should be given this pretty plant as its less obvious neighbors, the grasses and similar plants, are the true cause of any allergic reactions we might have. Commonly flowering in wet places in mid-summer, the plant forms a yellow-brown ball of disc flowers surrounded by drooping, yellow, ray flowers which together form the composite flower. The plant itself is two to four feet high with long leaves on an often branched stem.

Balsamorhiza sagittata
SUNFLOWER FAMILY

BALSAMROOT

Growing in clumps or colonies the balsamroot is one of our earliest blooming sunflowers and is quite common on the open, rolling, foothill slopes above Ash Mountain and in Cedar Grove. The rind of the root contains a turpentine-like balsam substance but the heart of the root is edible and was eaten by the Indians and early pioneers. In Utah a similar species is called Mormon biscuit.

Lotus oblongifolius
LEGUME FAMILY

MEADOW LOTUS

Meadow lotus is the most showy representative in Sequoia and Kings Canyon of the group often called bird's foot trefoil. It is abundant in moist, grassy places along streams, around mountain springs and in meadows. Meadows in the Giant Forest and Grant Grove areas are good places to find this species.

This clover-like perennial is particularly important to wildlife as forage and for its seeds, which are important to quail and small rodents.

Aquilegia pubescens
BUTTERCUP FAMILY

SIERRA COLUMBINE

To the summer back country hiker, the long spurred flowers of this plant brighten the dry rocky slopes of mountain passes and peaks up to elevations of 12,000 feet. The brilliantly colored flowers are also attractive to hummingbirds because of the abundance of nectar in the long hollow spurs.

Another species, *A. formosa*, with striking red flowers is found at lower elevations.

Mariposa Lily   *May–July*

Mountain Misery   *May–July*

Buck Brush   *March–May*

Thimbleberry   *March–August*

Sierra Star Tulip   *May—August*

Calochortus venustus
LILY FAMILY

MARIPOSA LILY

There are many species of mariposa lily in California, all of them striking in appearance. The scientific name of the species means "charming grass," while the common name, mariposa, is Spanish for "butterfly." This combination, charming butterfly, is appropriate, as the large, cup-shaped flowers come in many colors, mostly white, but also red, pink, purple, lilac and rarely yellow.

Bees and flies are attracted in great numbers to this slender stemmed flower of the dry open slopes and flats. As in the case of the brodiaeas' corms or roots, the Indians' notion with respect to Calochortus bulbs was that they were an edible gift of the gods.

Rubus parviflorus
ROSE FAMILY

THIMBLEBERRY

This leafy, thornless shrub, with large maple-like leaves, is a common sight along streams and in damp open woods of the yellow pine forest. Birds are particularly prominent among the long list of wildlife users of this plant, but for humans the scarlet, raspberry-like fruit is disappointing to the taste for it is composed mostly of seeds. Sometimes it is called white flowering raspberry.

Chamaebatia foliolosa
ROSE FAMILY

MOUNTAIN MISERY

Mountain misery or bear clover is a low, spreading shrub which forms thick mats under the pines of the dry yellow pine forest. On warm days such areas are full of the strong odor of witchhazel that comes from this low shrub. The feathery leaves are fern-like, but the small white flowers are shaped like single roses showing that it is a member of the rose family.

Indians used parts of the plant to brew a medicinal tea. More recently people outside the parks have tried, with little success, to remove this tenacious plant, which should be left in most areas to control erosion.

Ceanothus cuneatus
BUCKTHORN FAMILY

BUCK BRUSH

Among the most cheerful sights of a California spring is the blooming of the Ceanothus. From one end of the state to the other this characteristic shrub of the chaparral, in some of its many forms, spreads sheets of fragrant bloom in blue, lavender, or shining white on mountain slopes, canyon sides and open ridges. About 9 different species of Ceanothus can be found in Sequoia and Kings Canyon National Parks.

The name buck brush refers to the frequent browsing on leaves and stems by deer. The bushes also give shelter and provide nest sites for birds. The flowers of most species have the peculiar property of producing an abundant and cleansing lather when rubbed in water. Both bark and roots have been used as a home remedy for malaria, "catarrah," and as a treatment for spleen and liver conditions.

Calochortus minimus
LILY FAMILY

SIERRA STAR TULIP

This low-growing plant lives near the edges of moist meadows at middle elevations and arises from a small sweet bulb that was used as food by the Indians.

This species, one of more than seven in Sequoia and Kings Canyon National Parks, is easily distinguishable from all others as it is the only one with flowers on very short stalks. The stalks are so short that the plant appears to be one to three relatively large white flowers with a few long, thin sleeves.

Yucca   *May–June*

Corn Lily   *July–August*

Miner's Lettuce   *February–May*

Jimson Weed   *April–October*

Fivespot   *April—August*

Yucca whipplei
LILY FAMILY

YUCCA

The name, Our Lord's Candle, was given to this tall showy member of the Lily family by the early Spanish padres. Occasionally attaining a height up to 18 feet, this late spring blooming plant was given much use by the early Indians. The fibers from its leaves were used to hang meat to dry, were woven into coarse cloth and moccasins and braided into ropes and cords. The seeds provided food and the roots were used for making soap.

The plant is several years old before it is ready to flower, but the flower stalk, resembling a giant asparagus shoot, once started, grows with great rapidity. After the plant bears flowers and fruits, it dies and the dead stalks remain standing, sometimes for years.

Other common names include Spanish dagger or bayonet and lily of the desert.

Veratrum californicum
LILY FAMILY

CORN LILY

Corn lily is also called skunk cabbage because of the similarity of the young growth to that of the skunk cabbage of the northwest, which truly deserves the name. The two plants are in two very different families.

These 3 foot high plants have large, parallel-veined leaves and form dense patches in wet meadows. A corn-like tassel of flowers forms in late summer. The roots and young shoots are poisonous to livestock but are seldom eaten. Insects eat the leaves and the Indians used the plant as a remedy for many illnesses.

Claytonia perfoliata
PURSLANE FAMILY

MINER'S LETTUCE

These dainty succulent herbs are said to have earned the name miner's lettuce when used as salad plants by early pioneers, miners and Indians who ate the fleshy, tender leaves green or cooked. A tea was also made from the plant and used as a laxative.

The miner's lettuce is one of our most abundant springtime plants of shady and moist areas. When ripe, the shiny black seeds provide an important source of food for our western songbirds.

Datura wrightii
NIGHTSHADE FAMILY

JIMSON WEED

This bush-like foothill plant, with a densely prickly fruit and huge, trumpet-shaped flowers, contains a virulent narcotic poison. The flowers are a dazzling white in the morning but turn a delicate lavender-blue and close later in the day.

Indian tribes had a number of uses for the plant when performing their ceremonial rites, but the plant was always employed with great caution because of its poisonous qualities.

Other common names include sacred datura, moon lily and thorn-apple.

Nemophila maculata
WATERLEAF FAMILY

FIVESPOT

Fivespot is a flower of moist meadows and flats below 7,500 feet. This charming, low, spreading plant blooms in the spring with large flowers. Each flower petal has a large purple spot at its tip and because of this it has also been named calico flower and spotted nemophila.

The word Nemophila means "lover of the groves" and refers to the preference of many members of this group for wooded areas.

Sierra Rein Orchis   *May–August*

Popcorn Flower   *March–May*

California Buckeye   *May–June*

Indian Milkweed   *May–August*

Ranger's Buttons   *July–August*

Platanthera leucostachys
ORCHID FAMILY

SIERRA REIN ORCHIS

At first, one would not recognize the Sierra rein orchis as a member of the orchid family, but a close inspection reveals that the ½ inch long flowers are truly miniature orchids. The fragrant flowers are on delicate spikes and grace wet meadows in mid-summer.

While the rein orchis and coral root orchid are common and frequently seen, most other members of the orchid family are more rare. The green orchid, *Piperia unalascensis,* of dry areas, flowers after its leaves have dried. Rattlesnake plaintain, *Goodyera oblongifolia*, with its large mottled leaves, looks quite unlike an orchid and the rare saprophytic phantom orchid, *Cephalanthera austinae*, is waxy white with no leaves.

Asclepias eriocarpa
MILKWEED FAMILY

INDIAN MILKWEED

There are seven species of milkweed in the parks, all with heads of small flowers but with differing foliage. Milkweed is usually found in disturbed areas such as on road banks at the low and middle elevations of the parks. This plant can be recognized by its unusually shaped flowers, white hairy leaves and thick pods full of silky seeds.

The stems of milkweed furnished a strong fiber which was used by the Indians for making nets, rope and cloth. Poisonous juices from the plants are incorporated into the bodies of some insects, such as the monarch butterfly, which feed upon the plant. The poisonous juices protect these insects from predators.

Plagiobothrys tenellus
BORAGE FAMILY

POPCORN FLOWER

In early spring, as one drives through the foothills approaching the parks, meadows and grassy slopes give the appearance of being covered with popcorn or a light snow fall. A close relative to the forget-me-not, the small, white popcorn flower is responsible for this effect. When observed singly it is not very showy but its habit of blossoming by the thousands gives us a spectacle not soon forgotten.

Aesculus californica
BUCKEYE FAMILY

CALIFORNIA BUCKEYE

The California buckeye blooms early and sheds its large palmate leaves as soon as the soil dries in summer. In spring, spikes of many white flowers cover this small tree. In late summer and fall each spike is replaced by 1 to 2 large nuts in leathery coats.

Indians used the crushed, unripe seeds in streams to stupify fish. They also leached and roasted the nuts to prepare them as food when their acorn supply ran low or the acorn crop was poor. The California buckeye is closely related to the eastern horsechestnuts and buckeyes.

Sphenosciadium capitellatum
CARROT FAMILY

RANGER'S BUTTONS

This thick-rooted perennial is a close relative of cow parsnip and is sometimes confused with it but differs in having small, tight flower clusters. Ranger's buttons will be found along most of the water courses and swampy areas in the two parks, up to elevations of 10,500 feet. Other common names include swamp white heads and button parsnip.

Western Azalea   *April–August*

Pinedrops   *June–August*

Cow Parsnip   *April–July*

Pinemat Manzanita   *May–July*

Labrador Tea   *June–August*

Rhododendron occidentale
HEATH FAMILY

WESTERN AZALEA

No visitor can miss the beautiful flowers and honeysuckle odor of the western azalea. In early summer these handsome deciduous shrubs can be seen in the Sequoia groves of the General Grant Grove area and along other middle elevation streams and meadows. In Sequoia National Park the azalea is found near the Atwell Mill Grove.

The foliage is said to be poisonous to livestock but this is not a problem in the national parks. The azalea is a relative of the beautiful rhododendron of coastal California and of cultivated azaleas and rhododendrons.

Pterospora andromedea
HEATH FAMILY

PINEDROPS

You may occasionally see this peculiar plant in the rich soil of the ponderosa pine forest. The single reddishbrown stalk is generally sticky with a substance much like the pitch of pine trees. When mature the tall dark red stems often persist in a dried state until the following season.

Most plants manufacture their own food through a process called photosynthesis but this is true only of those plants having green leaves and stems. Pinedrops has no green parts at all. Because it lacks chlorophyll, it cannot manufacture its own food; so it must live as a parasite on fungi associated with the roots of forest trees.

Heracleum lanatum
CARROT FAMILY

COW PARSNIP

One of the showiest members of the carrot family, this coarse perennial can be found in meadows and moist places in many plant communities. Named for Hercules because of its great size, the plant is relished by livestock and wildlife. The early Indians ate the tender leaves and stems and cooked the roots which taste like rutabaga. Spanish speaking New Mexicans applied the powdered root to the body to reduce fever and pain from rheumatism and rubbed the powder on the gums when teeth were loose.

Arctostaphylos nevadensis
HEATH FAMILY

PINEMAT MANZANITA

One of the most noticeable shrubs one sees on approaching or upon entering the parks is the manzanita. In Sequoia and Kings Canyon National Parks five species are found. All five are characterized by thick evergreen leaves, urn shaped flowers, and a smooth reddish bark, which is their most prominent characteristic.

Winter visitors will see and smell the fragrant flowers of the sticky manzanita, *A. viscida*, as they pass through the foothill country. It grows up to 8 feet in height. As elevation increases, the bush-sized green leaf manzanita, *A. patula*, and pinemat manzanita, pictured here, will be found.

The Spanish name, manzanita, refers to the small green berries which are shaped like little apples. In summer the birds, squirrels, and even bear prize these fruits for foods as did the Monache Indians in this area.

Ledum glandulosum
HEATH FAMILY

LABRADOR TEA

Our Labrador tea is a low shrub of higher elevations. It is found in boggy and wet places near streams and lakes. The clusters of small flowers have a bitter fragrance when blooming in July. Tea made from the leathery leaves was used as a cure for rheumatism. In the past sheepmen claimed that, like other members of the heath family, it poisoned livestock. This species is not the true Labrador tea of the far north.

Blue Elderberry *June–September*

Yarrow *June–September*

Mountain Dogwood *April–July*

Shinleaf *June–August*

Sambucus mexicana
HONEYSUCKLE FAMILY

BLUE ELDERBERRY

This elderberry forms a bush or small tree in open areas. In late summer, the clusters of flat topped flowers turn into large masses of blue-black berries. Bear and many other animals eat the berries, and the foliage is often heavily browsed by deer.

This plant has had many uses. The Indians made a drink of the berries and also stored them for winter use. Spanish-speaking Californians made a tea as a cold remedy, and lately the berries have found their way into jelly, pies, and wine. The leaves and stems are poisonous and should not be mixed with the edible fruit. Other species are found at both higher and lower elevations.

Cornus nuttallii
DOGWOOD FAMILY

MOUNTAIN DOGWOOD

The Pacific or mountain dogwood flower appears superficially to be a single large blossom but is actually a dense cluster of small, greenish-white blossoms surrounded by 4 to 6 petal-like, white bracts. Closely resembling the eastern flowering dogwood, *C. florida*, these greenish-white blossoms mature into red, fleshy fruits in late summer and are valuable to wildlife.

The wood is hard, tough and close-grained and is used in the making of bobbins and shuttles for weaving and in cabinet work.

Another species, the creek dogwood, *C. stolonifera*, can be found along streams and in swampy areas.

Achillea a. millefolium
SUNFLOWER FAMILY

YARROW

Yarrow was named after Achilles for he is thought to have been the first to use it as medicine. It has been used for centuries to stop blood flow from wounds and to treat colds and fever. Sometimes reaching 2 feet in height, the plant can be recognized by its narrowly divided leaves, heads of small flowers and its aromatic odor. Another common name, milfoil, refers to the supposed thousand divisions of the leaves. Other species occur higher and lower, but this plant is found at middle elevations in damp places.

Pyrola picta
HEATH FAMILY

SHINLEAF

The leathery evergreen leaves, sometimes with prominent white veins, make this plant noticeable long before the fragrant waxy flowers appear.

The name shinleaf was given this plant long ago because English peasants used the leaves for plasters on blisters and sores. Look for it in forested areas along park trails during summer.

Chinese Houses   ***March–June***

Snow Plant   ***May–July***

Scarlet Monkeyflower   ***April–October***

Red Heather   ***July–August***

Lewis Monkeyflower   ***June—September***

Collinsia heterophylla
FIGWORT FAMILY

CHINESE HOUSES

In wooded areas of the foothills, either in open sunny spots or in dense shade where moisture still lingers, we find one of our loveliest spring-blooming plants. The delicate, usually many storied, blossoms arranged in crowded circles at intervals along the stem suggest the flaring roof lines of Chinese architecture, hence the name Chinese houses.

Sarcodes sanguinea
HEATH FAMILY

SNOW PLANT

The snow plant is one of the earliest spring flowers to take advantage of the abundant moisture left by melting snowbanks. One would infer, from the popular name, that it blooms in the snow, which is not true, except in the sense that a snowstorm out of season, coming after the development of the flowers, may temporarily surround it or even cover it with a snowy mantle.

Like many other members of the wintergreen family, the snow plant is a saprophyte. It does not manufacture its own food as plants with chlorophyll do. Its roots do not come into contact with the soil at all but are covered with a filamentous mat of microscopic fungus, which in return for board and lodging gathers nutriment from the earth for its host.

This widespread plant is supposedly poisonous but the Indians used the plant by drying it and then making a powder, which they made into a wash for ulcers, sore mouth and toothache.

Mimulus cardinalis
FIGWORT FAMILY

SCARLET MONKEYFLOWER

The scarlet monkeyflower, with its bright velvety blossoms, favors streamsides and damp places of shady canyons and can be found in these places through most of the summer months. This species, 2 to 4 feet high with flowers 1 to 2 inches long, is one of the largest and showiest of all the monkeyflowers occuring within the two parks.

Its scarlet, sometimes yellowish flowers, appear during the first year of growth and are favored by hummingbirds.

Phyllodoce breweri
HEATH FAMILY

RED HEATHER

Red heather forms carpets of bright flowers soon after the snow banks melt. This low, evergreen shrub is found in patches of wet, acid soil in rocky areas around the margins of high mountain meadows and lakes. Wiry branches are covered by narrow, rigid leaves and topped by brilliant, bell-shaped flowers.

This common plant has given its name to jewel-like Heather Lake on the north slope of Alta Peak in Sequoia National Park.

Mimulus lewisii
FIGWORT FAMILY

LEWIS MONKEYFLOWER

The large showy blossoms, borne in pairs on slender stalks, make the Lewis or pink monkeyflower one of the most beautiful of all flowers. Favoring streambanks and seepage areas it can be found at a wide range of elevations. The scarlet monkeyflower, *M. cardinalis*, can also be found in similar habitats but is a much larger plant and its flowers are a more intense shade of red.

This plant was scientifically named for Meriweather Lewis of the Lewis and Clark expedition.

Farewell To Spring   *May–August*

Sierra Lessingia   *July–October*

Pussy Paws   *May–August*

Western Redbud   *February–April*

Alpine Phlox   *May–August*

Clarkia dudleyana
EVENING PRIMROSE FAMILY

FAREWELL TO SPRING

After grasses and other herbs have turned brown with the approach of summer, the bright blossoms of this plant, and other similar appearing plants in the group *Clarkia*, continue to brighten park roadsides. All bloom about the same time and all are commonly referred to as farewell to spring. They are scientifically named in honor of Captain Clark of the Lewis and Clark expedition.

Indians collected the seeds of some clarkias, dried, parched and pulverized them and ate the meal dry or with acorn meal.

Lessingia leptoclada
SUNFLOWER FAMILY

SIERRA LESSINGIA

The slender, erect leaves of lessingia are branched above and have scattered, small, wooly leaves. Small flowers cover these plants making the mass effect one of soft color on drying hillsides.

Lessingia is often observed late in the summer at the dry lower margins of the yellow pine forest. It occurs below 6,000 feet and is commonly seen in the Hume Lake, Indian Basin and Cedar Grove areas.

Calyptridium umbellatum
PURSLANE FAMILY

PUSSY PAWS

Pussy paws is very abundant in the Sierra from early summer onward. It is most often found upon dry, rocky or sandy soils, often hugging the ground. At moderate altitudes the plant may form a rosette at least 10 inches wide, but as the elevation increases, (up to 13,000 feet) the size of the plant decreases to 2 inches or less in width. The name pussy paws is appropriate, for if one looks at the dense, overlapping, headlike clusters of flowers, they resemble the fuzzy toes of a cat. Several other species of *Calyptridium* occur within the parks, but this one is most commonly seen.

The plant produces tiny black seeds that are much relished by the chipmunks who harvest them with amazing skill, packing their cheek pouches with them and carrying them off to their granaries for winter consumption.

Cercis occidentalis
PEA FAMILY

WESTERN REDBUD

No springtime traveler to the parks can miss the striking redbud of the foothills. Masses of flowers varying in color from light pink to reddish-purple cover the stems in late winter and early spring. The flowers form before the leaves and are replaced by clusters of long, purplish pods among the heart-shaped, green leaves.

The flexible twigs were used by the Indians in making their intricate baskets. Redbud is also called Judas tree because legend tells us that the flowers turned from white to red when Judas hanged himself from the limbs of a related species found in Israel.

Phlox diffusa
PHLOX FAMILY

ALPINE PHLOX

When this plant is flowering, it is a conspicuous mat of prickly, green leaves covered by pink to white flowers. A perennial, it can become quite woody at its base. These dense mats are common in gravelly or rocky areas at middle and high elevations.

A similar species, *P. dispersa*, is found in areas above timberline, and showy phlox, *P. speciosa* ssp. *occidentalis*, is found on rocky slopes of middle elevations.

Geranium   *July–August*

Swamp Onion   *July–September*

Bleeding Heart   *March–July*

Crimson Columbine   *April–August*

California Indian Pink   *March—August*

Allium validum
LILY FAMILY

SWAMP ONION

Wild onions can easily be recognized by their odor. Many hikers use this species to add flavor to their foods just as they were once used by the Monache Indians who inhabited this area. Swamp onions are found as large clumps in wet meadows at high elevations. The showy flowers form dense heads above long grass-like leaves.

There are other smaller species found in dry situations, some with good flavor and others with a garlic-like taste to the tiny, white or pink bulbs.

Aquilegia formosa
CROWFOOT FAMILY

CRIMSON COLUMBINE

This plant, native to nearly all states, is found in moist situations along streams and in meadows at middle elevations. The scientific name, *Aquilegia*, is probably from the Latin word for eagles and refers to the fancied resemblance of the hooked spurs of the petals to eagle's talons.

The roots, leaves and seeds had a variety of uses in the early days. The leaves were commonly used in lotions for sore mouths and throats, or boiled and eaten in the spring. Boiled roots were used in a tea to stop diarrhea and the Spaniards would eat a piece of the root in the morning on fast days. Ripe seeds were mashed, moistened and then rubbed into the hair to discourage lice.

Geranium richardsonii
GERANIUM FAMILY

GERANIUM

The long stems of this wild geranium hang on other plants in very wet places such as shady streamsides and meadows from 4,000 to 9,000 feet. This geranium is unlike its cultivated namesake in many ways. The garden geranium belongs to the genus *Pelargonium* and has many flowers on a thick stemmed plant with fleshy leaves. Our wild geranium has a few, pretty, white blossoms with pinkish veins and deeply divided leaves.

The name geranium is from the Greek word "geranos" meaning "a crane," in reference to the long beak which forms on the seed capsule.

Dicentra formosa
POPPY FAMILY

BLEEDING HEART

In damp, more or less shaded places, especially on the trail to Crystal Cave, we find this charming plant. The leaves are long stemmed and deeply dissected into numerous, delicate lobes while the flowers are heart shaped and pendant. At higher elevations in the parks another species of this plant can be found, *D. nevadensis*, with similar flowers.

Recently, this plant has been found to be dangerously poisonous to stock and is known as staggerweed in some localities.

Silene californica
PINK FAMILY

CALIFORNIA INDIAN PINK

Over a dozen species of *Silene* occur in this area but the California Indian Pink, also called catchfly or campion, is the most colorful. It is found in open, bushy or wooded places from early spring through the summer. The widely distributed perennial was made into a tea for aches, sprains and sores in pioneer days.

Another common species, at higher elevations, is *S. montana*, which has mostly white flowers.

Sierra Shooting Star   June–August

Yellow Throated Gilia   May–August

Pride of the Mountains   June–August

Purple Owl's Clover   March–May

California Fuchsia   August–October

Linanthus montanus
PHLOX FAMILY

YELLOW THROATED GILIA

Of the approximately 12 species of *Linanthus* that grow within the parks, the yellow throated gilia, or mustang clover, is probably the most commonly seen. It is found in dry, gravelly areas above 4,000 feet, where it grows in great profusion, in the Giant Forest, Lodge-pole and Grant Grove areas. This same plant also grows in the foothills below 4,000 feet where it may attain a height of a foot or more and exhibit white flowers, scarcely resembling the higher elevation form. It is also called Mustang Clover.

Castilleja exserta
FIGWORT FAMILY

PURPLE OWL'S CLOVER

During early spring in the foothills, on open fields and grassy slopes, the owl's clover forms sheets of brilliant color often covering hundreds of acres. Crowded in open spots or scattered individually throughout the grass, it is an important flower of the spring wildflower display.

Not actually a clover, owl's clover has also been named Escobita, Spanish for little "whisk broom."

Dodecatheon jeffreyi
PRIMROSE FAMILY

SIERRA SHOOTING STAR

Of the 6 different kinds of shooting stars that occur within the two parks, the Jeffrey shooting star is the one most frequently seen in meadows and moist areas in the Giant Forest and Grant Grove areas during the early summer months. The name shooting star aptly describes the way in which the petals flare backwards, much like the tail of a comet. Other names for shooting stars are mad violets, prairie pointer, rooster head, mosquito bill and bird bill.

Penstemon newberryi
FIGWORT FAMILY

PRIDE OF THE MOUNTAINS

Brightening the rocky areas along roads and trails at middle and high elevations is pride of the mountains. These perennial plants form somewhat woody clumps which are topped by tubular flowers. In late summer, patches of its deep color fill seemingly inhospitable nooks on rock ledges.

In the bearded flower opening, one flower part is flat and tongue-shaped, giving the name "beard-tongue" to plants of this group. These colorful flowers are pollinated by both butterflies and hummingbirds.

Epilobium canum
EVENING PRIMROSE FAMILY

CALIFORNIA FUCHSIA

California fuchsia forms low clumps in open rocky areas of the forest from low to high elevations. It obtained its name from the cultivated fuchsia because of the similarity of their tubular, scarlet flowers. The petals are two cleft and attract hummingbirds. For this reason it has also been called hummingbird's trumpet.

The plant is hairy and somewhat sticky. California fuchsia is one of the last plants to flower at middle elevations and forms brilliant clumps along the Generals Highway.

Indian Paintbrush   *May–September*

Elephant Heads   *June–August*

Showy Phlox   *April–June*

Pale Laurel   *June–August*

Sierra Gooseberry   *May–June*

Castilleja miniata
FIGWORT FAMILY

INDIAN PAINTBRUSH

Species of paintbrush are found at all elevations and in nearly all habitats, from wet meadows to dry banks and slopes. There are at least 11 species in the two parks, and many others in the western United States. This paintbrush is a common species along streams and in wet places at middle and high elevations in the Sierra Nevada.

What appear to be the true flowers are bright bracts or modified leaves that surround the inconspicuous flowers. These bracts form vividly colored spikes atop branches clothed by alternate leaves with wavy margins. Some species are partial parasites on the roots of other plants.

Pedicularis groenlandica
FIGWORT FAMILY

ELEPHANT HEADS

You will find this strange looking plant in wet meadows of alpine areas in July and August. Upon close observation of an individual flower, we see that the peculiarly modified petals of the corolla resemble

the forehead, ears and waving trunk of an elephant.
Another species, *P. attollens*, often found growing with the above is similar to it in general structure but its leaves are more dissected.

Phlox speciosa ssp. *occidentalis*
PHLOX FAMILY

SHOWY PHLOX

Of some 50 species of phlox occurring in North America, about 8 occur within the boundaries of Sequoia-Kings Canyon National Parks. Most of these occur at higher elevations and are not often seen except by the backcountry hiker. But the showy phlox, with its brilliantly colored flowers, occurs along road-

sides, on rocky hillsides and wooded slopes in April, May and June.
Many species of phlox are extensively cultivated, producing a great variety of forms with a wide range of colors.

Kalmia polifolia var. *microphylla*
HEATH FAMILY

PALE LAUREL

On the margins of many high country lakes, where the soil is moist, we find the pale laurel, one of our smallest evergreen shrubs with dark green leaves. Often growing at elevations as high as 12,000 feet, it frequently forms mats covering large areas. Quite often

it can be found growing in association with red heather, *Phyllodoce breweri*, with which it is often confused. The flower of pale laurel is open and saucer-shaped while that of heather is urn-shaped.

Ribes roezlii
GOOSEBERRY FAMILY

SIERRA GOOSEBERRY

In early spring, at various elevations, the rose colored flowers of the Sierra gooseberry begin to appear along park roadsides. The fruit, green in early summer, turns a brilliant red in late summer. Distinguishable from currants by the lack of spines or prickles on the stem, the fruit of the wild gooseberry is very disappointing as its large, spiny berries are composed mostly of skin and seeds. But for wildlife, such as songbirds, ground

squirrels, chipmunks and other animals, the fruits have considerable value.
Gooseberries and currants are alternate hosts of the white pine blister rust and efforts have been made in the past to exterminate them in places where there are commercially valuable white pine forests. Attempts are now being made to develop varieties of white pine which are resistant to the fungus.

Velvety Stickseed   *June–August*

Fireweed   *March–August*

Sierra Primrose   *July–August*

Rock Fringe   *July–September*

Indian Warrior   *January–June*

Hackelia velutina
BORAGE FAMILY

VELVETY STICKSEED

Velvety stickseed flowers from June to August in open places of middle and high elevation forest. Identification of this plant can be confusing because it produces either pink or sky-blue flowers. These flowers are in clusters atop the velvety plants. The plant gets its name stickseed because of the prickly fruits which stick to and are carried by animals and people. There are other stickseeds in the borage family which distribute their seed in this manner.

Another species, *H. sharsmithii*, is found only in alpine areas near Mount Whitney.

Epilobium angustifolium
EVENING PRIMROSE FAMILY

FIREWEED

The fireweed is sometimes referred to as willow herb because of its willow-like leaves. It is frequently the first plant to come in after a forest fire and in other disturbed areas, but it is also fond of meadows and wet areas in both parks. It can be found in such places during mid and late summer.

The plant, one of the most widely disseminated wildflowers in the world, has had various uses through the ages. In Europe and Asia its young shoots were eaten like asparagus, in England the leaves were used as a tea adulterant, and in Canada the young leaves and stems were used as a pot herb.

Primula suffrutescens
PRIMROSE FAMILY

SIERRA PRIMROSE

Sierra primrose forms a beautiful, rose-purple display as a border to granite boulders above timberline. Only hikers will find this alpine plant with its flowers standing on stalks above a basal tuft of leaves. Because of the short growing season at high elevations, this primrose blooms soon after the protective snow banks melt.

The name primus means spring in Latin and refers to the early flowering of members of this group. Unlike the cultivated primrose, this species is a perennial, not an annual.

Epilobium obcordatum
EVENING PRIMROSE FAMILY

ROCK FRINGE

Rock fringe, also called alpine willow herb, is found in areas above timberline often as high as 13,000 feet, growing in rock crevices and about rocks. The plant is quite small but has large, showy flowers about an inch across.

Sierra primrose, *Primula suffrutescens*, looks similar and grows in similar areas but is in a different family.

Pedicularis densiflora
FIGWORT FAMILY

INDIAN WARRIOR

This plant is called Indian warrior as the crimson flowers, which are borne in a dense spike at the end of a stout stem, seem to resemble the stiff headdress of feathers worn by Indian chiefs. It was once thought that cattle had more lice after eating plants of this group; thus the genus or group was named, *Pedicularis*, the Latin term for lice. This in turn brought about another common name for this group, lousewort.

Fond of dry slopes below 6,000 feet, the louseworts are thought to be partially parasitic on roots of other plants. Until the flowers appear, the foliage of this plant is often mistaken for fern fronds.

Chia   *March–June*

Wild Hyacinth   *March–May*

Sky Pilot   *July–August*

Harvest Brodiaea   *April–July*

Baby Blue-Eyes   *February–June*

Salvia columbariae
MINT FAMILY

CHIA

For the early California Indians, the ripe seeds of the chia had a variety of uses. The seeds, being very high in food value and easily digested, were gathered, parched and ground up into a powder. Having a nutty flavor, the powder was sometimes cooked later as a gruel, eaten in dry pinches or diluted with water to make a drink. In addition to being eaten, the seed paste was used as a poultice for gunshot wounds or used medicinally to soothe inflamed digestive organs. Look for it in open, dry areas in the foothills during early spring.

Brodiaea elegans
LILY FAMILY

HARVEST BRODIAEA

The first *Brodiaea* seen by any botanist seems to have been the harvest brodiaea, first collected in 1792. It is abundant on open or wooded plains, foothills and sometimes in wet meadows about the time of the hay harvest throughout the great central valley of California. By the time the plant is in full bloom, the leaves have usually withered and dried up.

Like other brodiaeas, the corms were eaten by the California Indians.

Dichelostemma capitatum
LILY FAMILY

WILD HYACINTH

Wild hyacinth is found in the foothills below the yellow pine forest and is the earliest blooming brodiaea of the many found in the two parks. Its fleshy corms have been eaten by Indians and other local residents. Indian women dug the corms with sharp pointed digging sticks of oak or mountain mahogany and ate the tiny morsels either raw or cooked. To cook them, a pit was dug and lined with heated rocks. After the corms were placed in layers separated by green leaves, the hole was covered with earth and a fire lighted on top. After a day or two, the pit was opened and the well steamed roots were ripe for eating, the sweeter for the long, slow cooking. They were considered best when gathered soon after the flowers had dried.

Polemonium eximium
PHLOX FAMILY

SKY PILOT

The backcountry traveler will see this striking plant which occurs only above 11,000 feet in the southern Sierra. This uncommon perennial can often be located by its strong, musky odor before the plant is seen. It is a rare treat to come upon the showy plant with delicate flowers clustered in heads atop 8 inch stems.

To find such a plant among the boulders above timberline attests to its amazing ability to adapt to the extreme environmental conditions of short growing season and lack of well developed soil.

Nemophila menziesii
WATERLEAF FAMILY

BABY BLUE-EYES

A very showy and abundant plant of the lowlands is the baby blue-eyes, often blooming in early February on moist, grassy slopes below 2500 feet. This species is one of the showiest of several species of *Nemophila* occurring in the parks.

Another more common species, often overlooked, is *N. pulchella* with small blue flowers.

Ithuriel's Spear   *April–June*

Bush Lupine   *March–June*

Wild Iris   *May–June*

Sierra Gentian   *July–September*

Blue Lips   *May–August*

ITHURIEL'S SPEAR

Tritelia laxa
LILY FAMILY

Light blue to white flowers atop a "spear" up to two feet in height makes this the most majestic of our brodiaeas.

The stem, straight like the spear borne by the angel Ithuriel, has given the common name "Ithuriel's spear," to this plant. Legend tells us that Ithuriel possessed a truth compelling spear. When

Satan went to the Garden of Eden to tempt Eve, angels Ithuriel and Zephron were sent to expel him.

The other common name, grass nut, indicates that its corm was highly prized by local Indians. Ithuriel's spear is often plentiful in road cuts at the lower elevations.

SIERRA GENTIAN

Gentianopsis holopetala
GENTIAN FAMILY

Handsome, terminal flowers attract attention to the gentians found in our middle and high elevation meadows. The single, colorful blossoms of the Sierra gentian are funnel-shaped and four-lobed, quite large for such a small plant.

The genus was named for Gentius, an ancient king, who is said to have discovered the medicinal

properties of these plants. The color of the medicine, gentian violet, is well known. This deep blue color is characteristic of 4 of the 6 species which occur in these parks.

A large relative, *Frasera*, has a spike of many green flowers and is found at the margins of high elevation meadows.

BUSH LUPINE

Lupinus albifrons
PEA FAMILY

Over 80 species of lupine in California can readily be recognized as a group by their spikes of flowers and leaves divided into many, often fuzzy, leaflets. This bush lupine is found in the foothills where it forms a 2 to 5 foot bush with silky leaves and flowers in a long spike.

The genus was named after the wolf, Lupus, because it was thought that these plants were destructive to soil. Actually, lupines are important both for control of erosion in loose soil and for enriching soil through nitrogen fixation.

WILD IRIS

Iris hartwegii
IRIS FAMILY

Iris means "rainbow" and Iris was the rainbow-winged messenger of the Greek gods. The irises are also called "flags" and are the "fleur-de-lis" of the French. Iris species hybridize easily and many varieties are cultivated as ornamentals.

This species has flowers varying in color from yel-

low and lavender to yellow and cream and is found on dry, wooded slopes. Another species, *I. missouriensis*, forms colonies in middle elevation meadows in early summer. Its 3 inch flowers have petals of light blue to white.

BLUE LIPS

Collinsia torreyi
FIGWORT FAMILY

A small plant, only a few inches high, the blue lips or blue-eyed Mary, often carpets roadside banks and flats in the Giant Forest and Grant Grove areas from May through mid-summer.

A variety of this species *C. torreyi* var. *wrightii* has flowers exactly the same in color and shape but so small they are barely visible.

Meadow Lupine *May–August*

Fiesta Flower *March–May*

Hansen's Delphinium *April–June*

Littleleaf Ceanothus *May–July*

Lupinus polyphyllus var. *burkei*
PEA FAMILY

MEADOW LUPINE

This lupine stands from 2 to 5 feet high in the margins of wet meadows and is one of the most luxuriant in flower and foliage of all sierran lupines. There are over 40 other kinds of lupine in the two parks.

The dramatically colorful spike of pea-like flowers contrasts with the yellow *senecios* of the middle elevation meadows in mid-summer. The dark, purplish-green leaves have from 5 to 9 leaflets. Fuzzy leaves and pods remain after the flowers have faded.

Pholistoma auritum var. *auritum*
WATERLEAF FAMILY

FIESTA FLOWER

A straggling plant of moist woods and canyon, the fiesta flower, with its lavender to purple blossoms, can be found blooming in the foothills during March through June. This sprawling annual, with flowers almost an inch in diameter, is equipped with prickles on the stems so that it clings to clothing.

Delphinium hansenii
BUTTERCUP FAMILY

HANSEN'S DELPHINIUM

Various parts of many members of the Ranunculaceae family, to which the larkspurs belong, are poisonous to man and other animals. But yellow buttercups and the usually deep blue larkspur and monkshood do much to beautify many sierran habitats.

Ceanothus parvifolius
BUCKTHORN FAMILY

LITTLELEAF CEANOTHUS

Whitethorn, deer brush, wild lilac, and various types of "mats" are common names that have been given to species of Californian members of the Ceanothus genus. This is one of the most beautiful, a low growing bush which grows in open areas of lower elevation forest. Other species are white or cream colored, but this has striking violet flowers.

REFERENCES

Abrams, L — *Illustrated Flora of the Pacific States*. Stanford University Press, California. vl,2,3, 1940.

Abrams, L. and Ferris, R. S. — *Illustrated Flora of the Pacific States*. Stanford University Press, California v4. 1960

Balls, E. K. — *Early Uses of California Plants*. University of California Press, Berkeley, California. 1972.

Clements, E. S. — *Flowers of Coast and Sierra*. H. W. Wilson Company, New York. 1928.

Hickman, J. C. — *The Jepson Manual Higher Plants of California*. U. C. Press. 1993.

Horn, E. L. — *Wildflowers 3, The Sierra Nevada*. The Touchstone Press, Beaverton, Oregon. 1976.

Kingsbury, J. M. — *Deadly Harvest*. Holt, Rinehart and Winston, San Francisco, California. 1956.

Morgenson, D. C. — *Yosemite Wildflower Trails*. Yosemite Natural History Association. 1976.

Munz, P. A. — *California Mountain Wildflowers*. University of California Press, Berkeley, California. 1963.

Munz, P. A. — *A Supplement To A California Flora*. University of California Press, Berkeley, California. 1968.

Munz, P. A. — *A Supplement To A California Flora*. University of California Press, Berkeley, California. 1965. (Reprint).

Niehaus, T. F. — *Sierra Wildflowers,* Mount Lassen to Kern Canyon. University of California Press, Berkeley, California. 1974.

Niehaus, T. F. and Ripper, Charles L. — *A Field Guide to Pacific States Wildflowers*. Houghton Mifflin Company, Boston. 1976.

Parsons, M. E. — *The Wildflowers of California*. California Academy of Sciences, San Francisco, California. 1959.

Pusateri, S. J. — *Flora of Our Sierran National Parks*. Carl & Irving Printers, Tulare, California. 1963.

Sauders, C. F. — *Western Wildflowers and Their Stories*. Doubleday, Doran and Co., Inc., New York. 1963.

Storer, T. I. and Usinger, R. L. — *Sierra Nevada Natural History*. University of California Press, Berkeley, California. 1963.

Sweet, M. — *Common Edible and Useful Plants of the West*. Naturegraph Company, Healdsburg, California. 1962.

Weeden, Norman F. — *A Sierra Nevada Flora*. Wilderness Press. 1996.

Wilson, Lynn, Jim and Jeff Nicholas — *Wildflowers of Yosemite*. Sierra Press Inc. 1994.

INDEX